SRA Open Court Reading

Heroes

SRA
A Division of The McGraw-Hill Companies
Columbus, Ohio

www.sra4kids.com

SRA/McGraw-Hill
A Division of The **McGraw·Hill** Companies

Copyright © 2002 by SRA/McGraw-Hill.

All rights reserved. Except as permitted under the United States Copyright Act, no part of this publication may be reproduced or distributed in any form or by any means, or stored in a database or retrieval system, without prior written permission from the publisher.

Printed in the United States of America.

Send all inquiries to:
SRA/McGraw-Hill
8787 Orion Place
Columbus, OH 43240-4027

ISBN 0-07-569927-3

   3 4 5 6 7 8 9 DBH 05 04 03 02

Smoke rose high in the sky. Joey rode his bike up the road to see why.

"Oh, no," said Joey. "The Nolans' home is burning, and I know that no one is home."

4

"Mom, smoke is coming from the Nolans' home," said Joey.

Mom spoke on the phone. "There is a fire at 222 Grove Road. Please hurry!"

The firefighters hurry, hurry, hurry! They slide on the pole. They put on their yellow coats and jump in the fire truck.

Joey sees the firefighters soak the Nolans' home. The water flow stops the fire. The Nolans' home is safe.

"Mom, those men and women are real heroes," says Joey.
"So are you, Joey," says Mom.